liz story

Management: Alan Oken Organization
Transcribed by Ned Ginsburg and Jim Tyler
Electronic Music Typesetting by Sheldon Music Service
Production Manager: Daniel Rosenbaum
Art Direction: Alisa Hill
Administration: Marianne Monroe
Director of Music: Mark Phillips

ISBN: 0-89524-480-2

Edited by Milton Okun

C O N T E N T S

ANA

Music by Liz Story

(2nd time)

To Coda I

D.C.(take 2nd ending)al Coda I

7

Coda I

D.C. al Coda II

Coda II

8

DEVOTION

Music by Liz Story

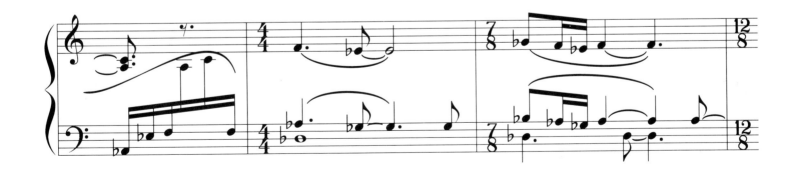

*12/8 and 9/8 in this piece remain in *duple* meter
 (the beat is subdivided by two).

11

FORGIVENESS

Music by Liz Story

Medium tempo

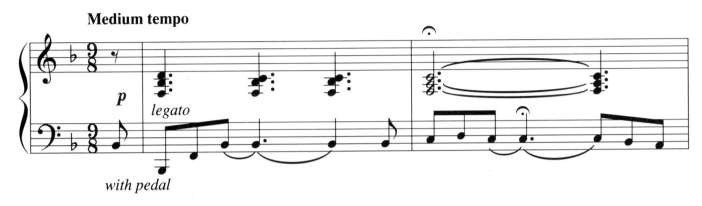

4th time to Coda III⊕

3rd time to Coda II⊕   2nd time to Coda I⊕

D.S. al Coda I 𝄋

Coda I
⊕

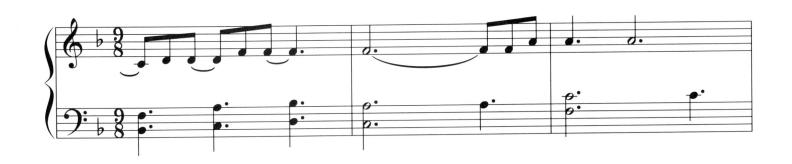

D.S. al Coda II 𝄋

Coda II

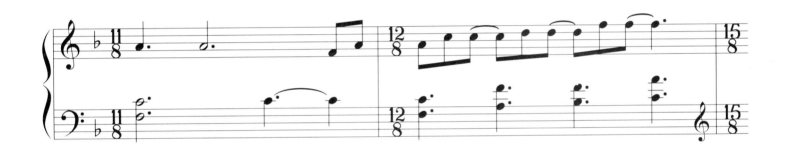

Coda III

FROG PARK

Music by Liz Story

First time twice;
Second time three times

To Coda ⊕

HERMES DANCE

Music by Liz Story

with pedal

sim.

mf

mp

sim.

D.S. (with repeat) al Coda

with pedal

mf

sim.

SOLID COLORS

Music by Liz Story

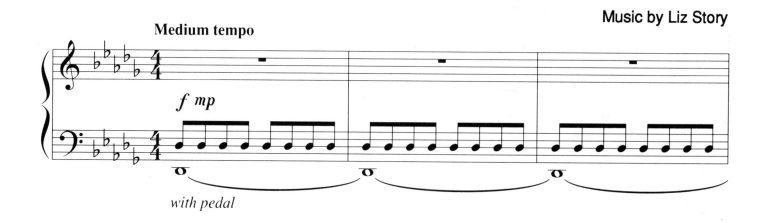

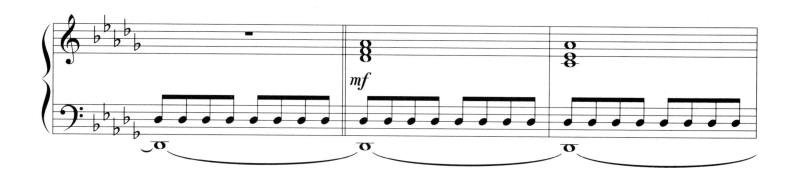

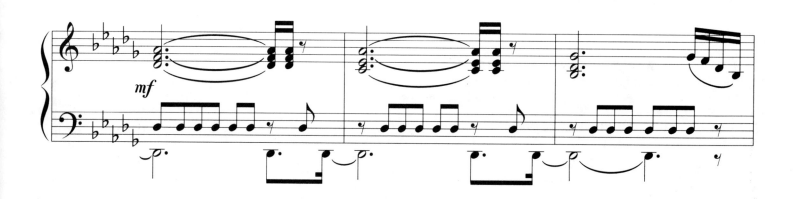

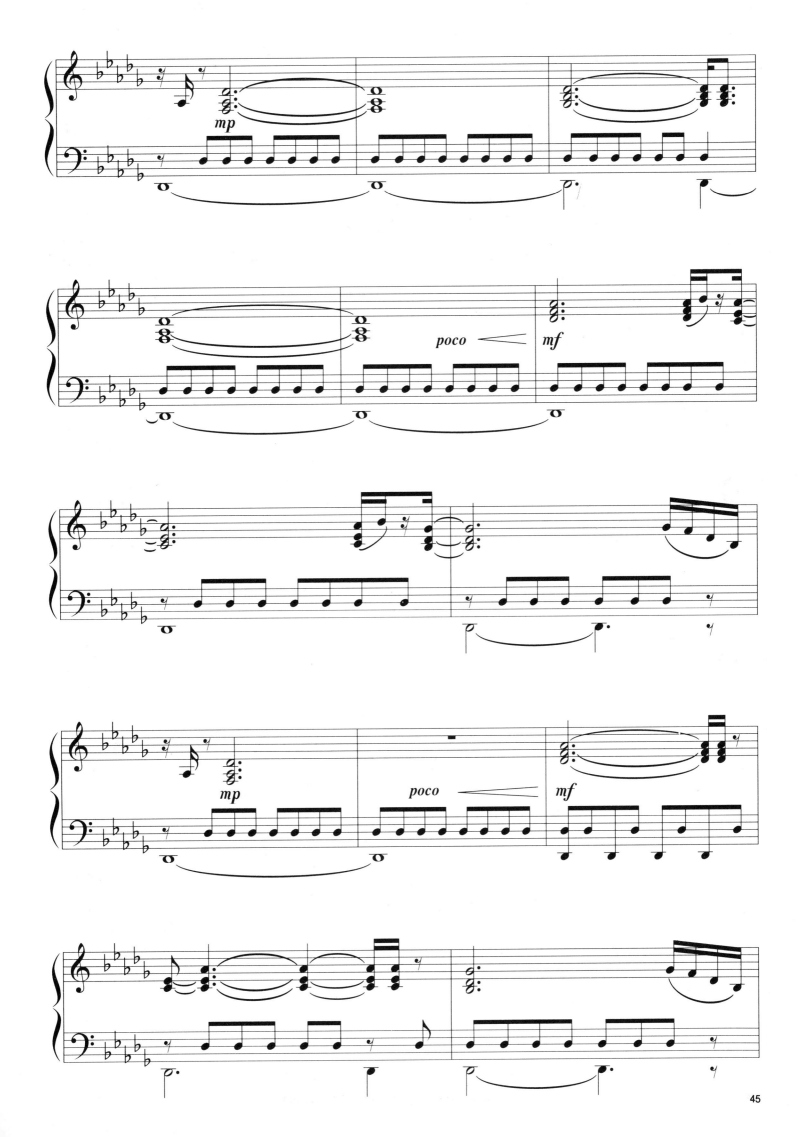

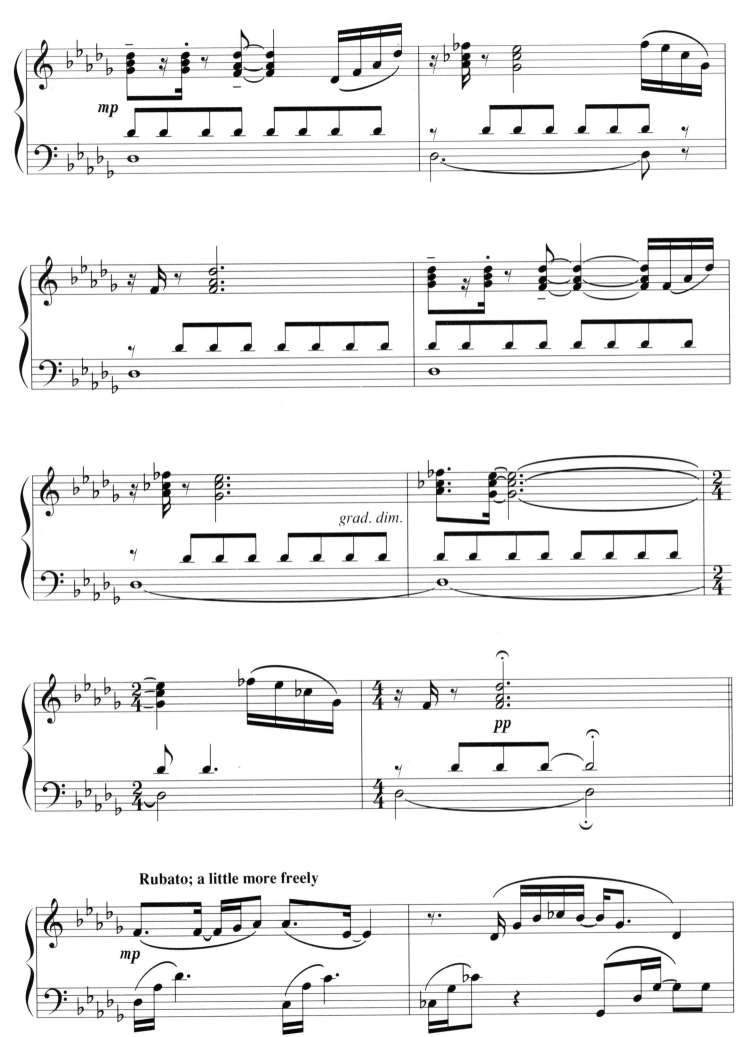

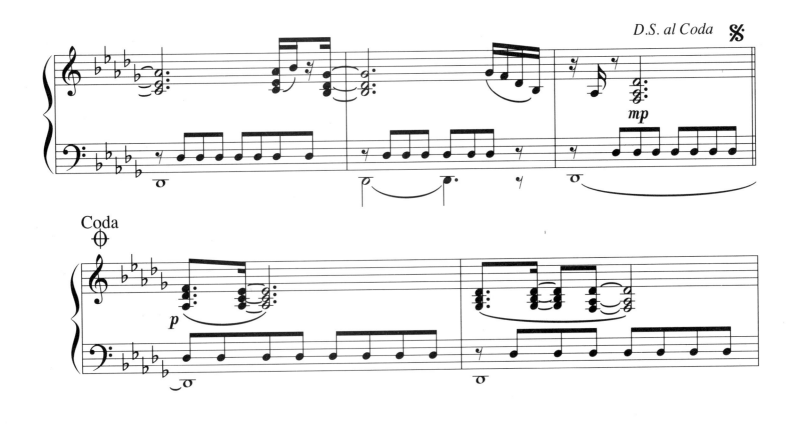

Coda

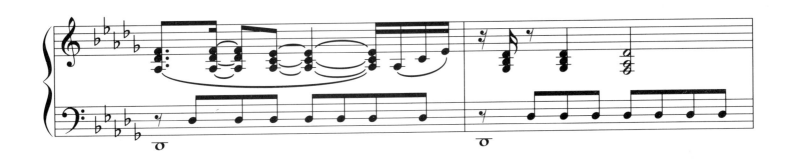

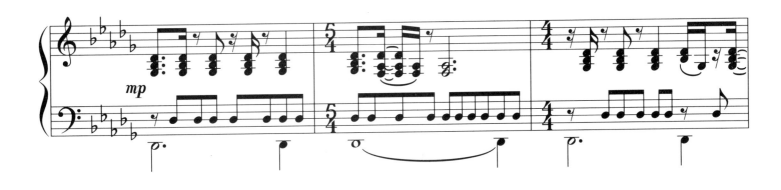

TEASED HAIR

Music by Liz Story

Medium tempo, Rag-like

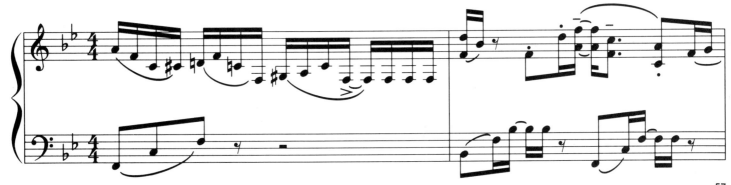

THINGS WITH WINGS

Music by Liz Story

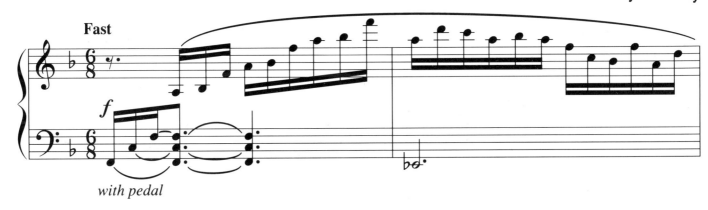

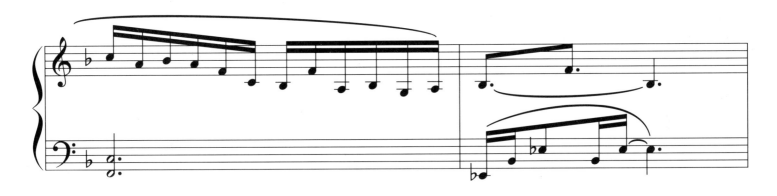

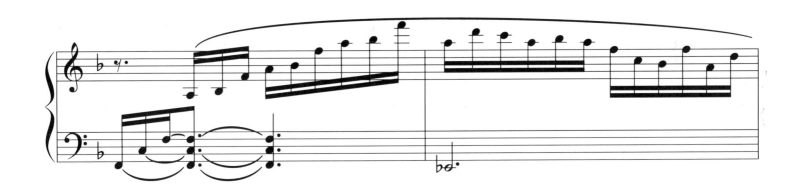

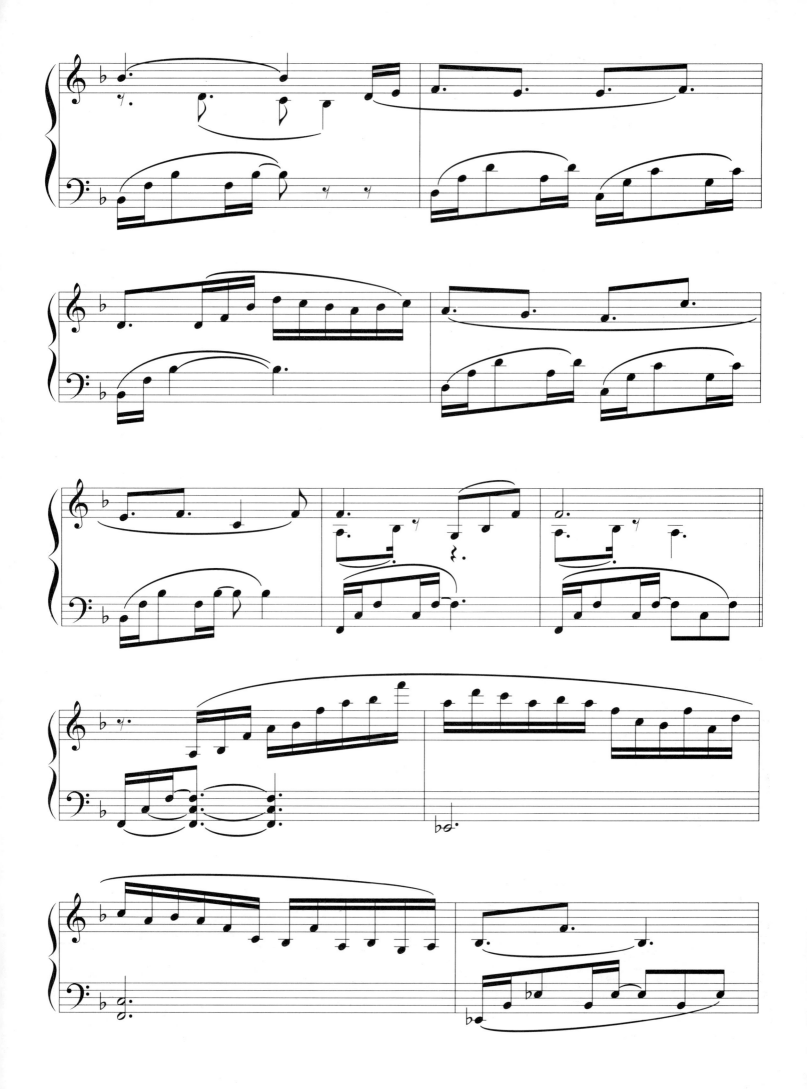

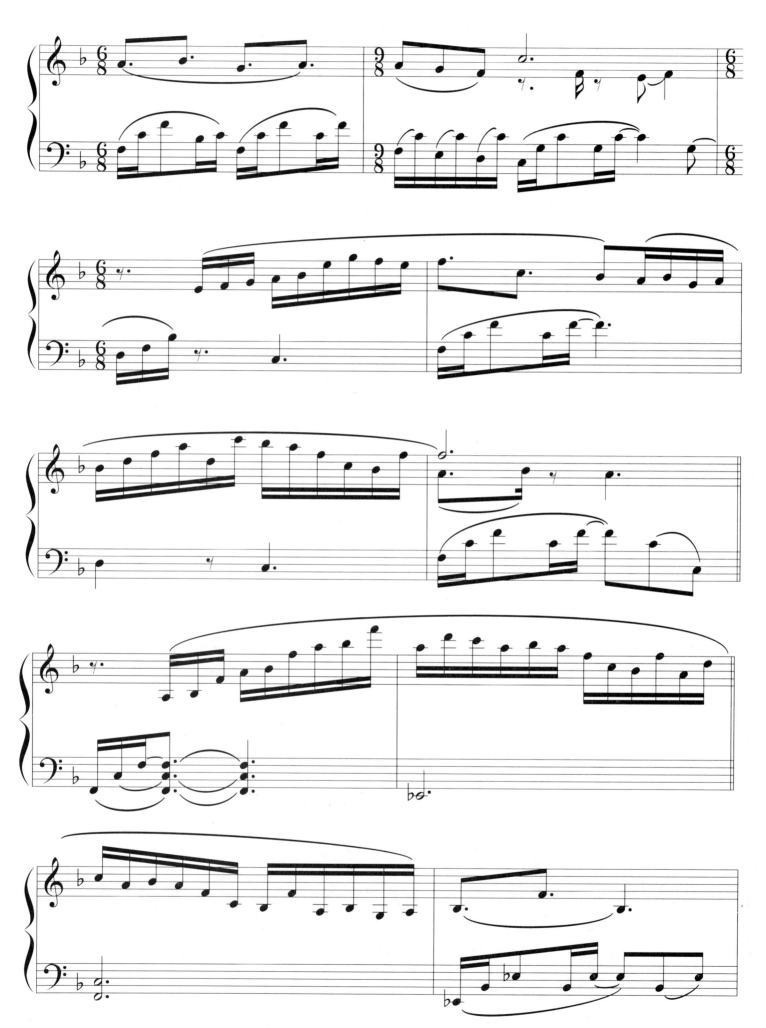

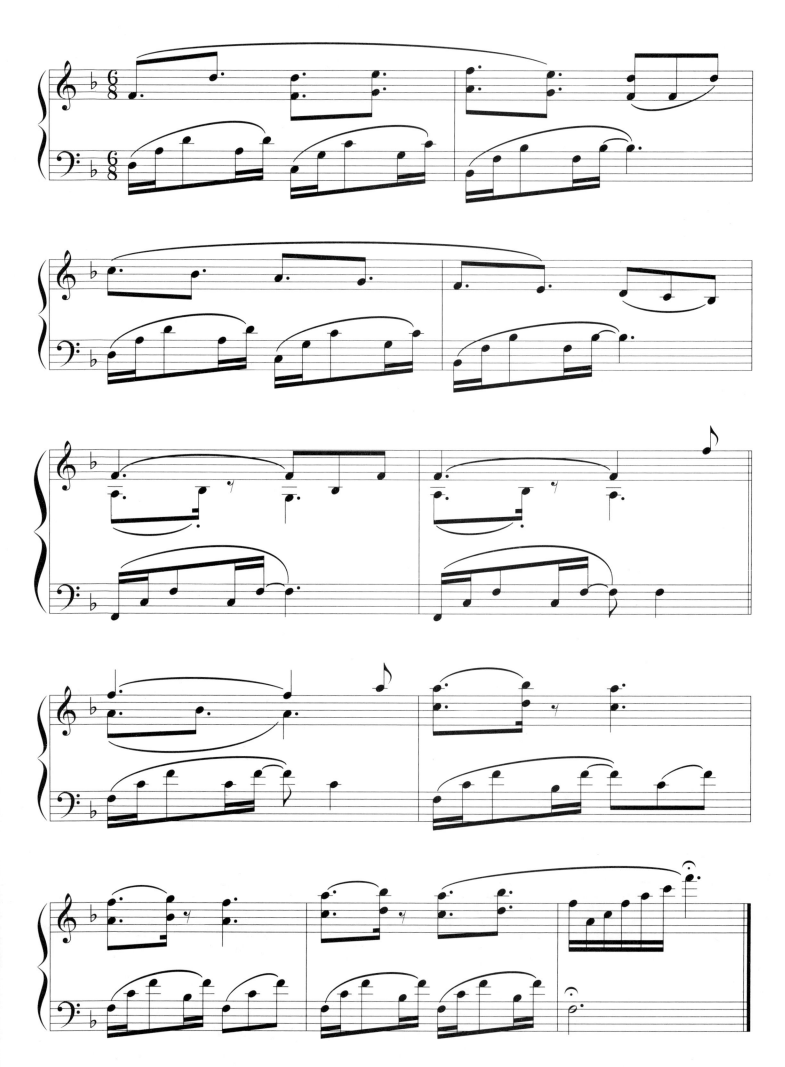

TOY SOLDIERS

Music by Liz Story

To Coda ⊕

72

D.S. al Coda 𝄋

Coda

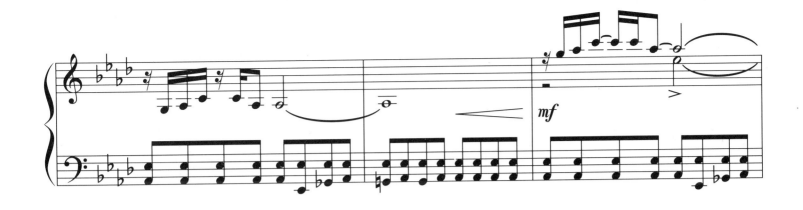

WEDDING RAIN

Music by Liz Story

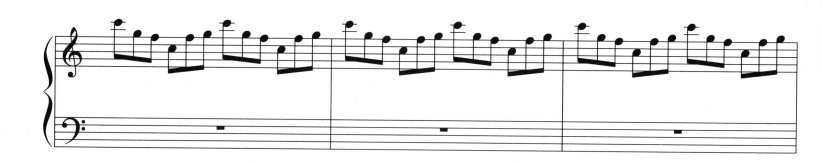

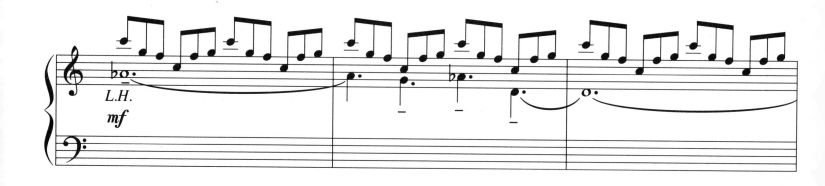

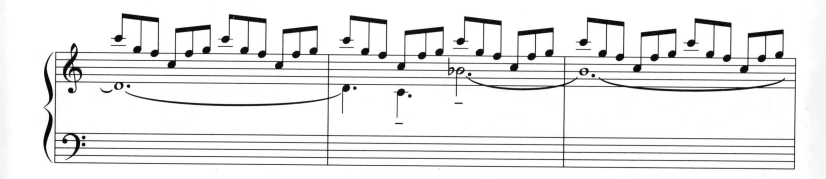

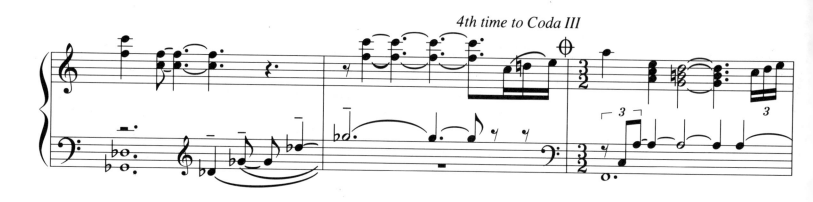

4th time to Coda III

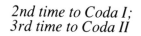

2nd time to Coda I;
3rd time to Coda II

espressivo

D.S. al Coda I

mp

Coda I

espressivo

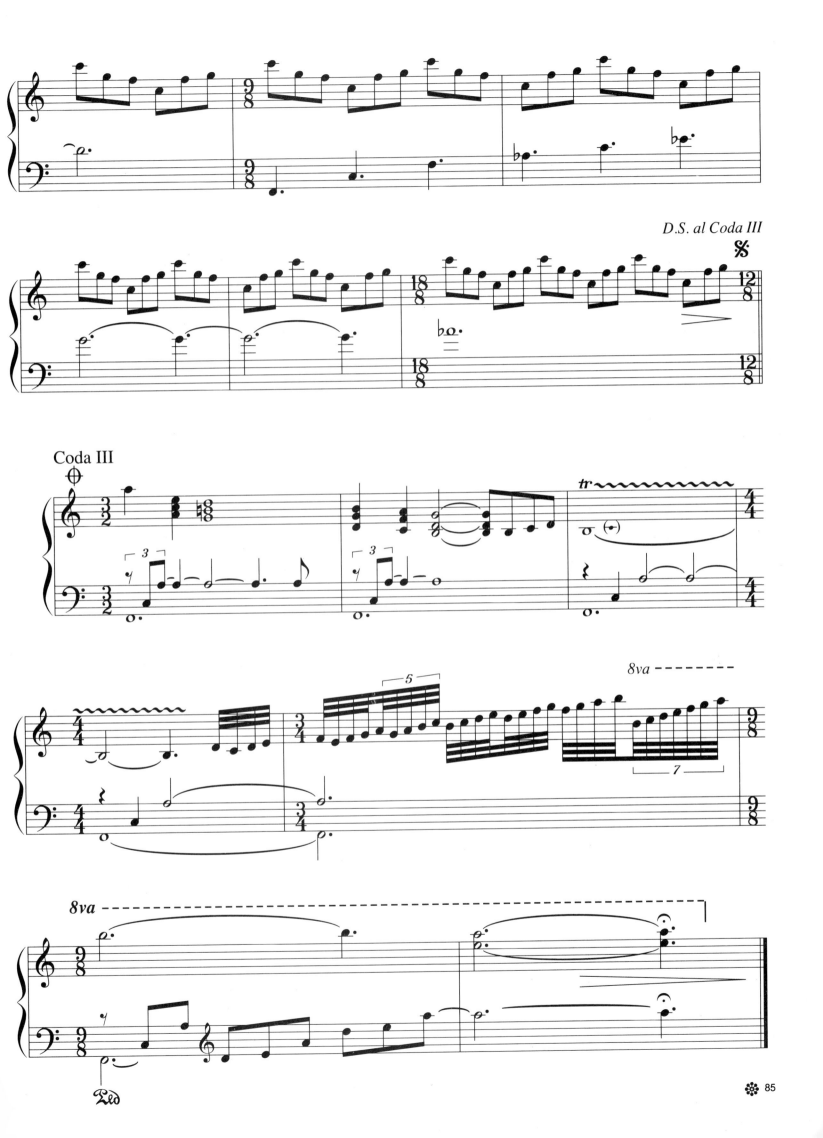

D.S. al Coda III

Coda III

WELCOME HOME

Music by Liz Story

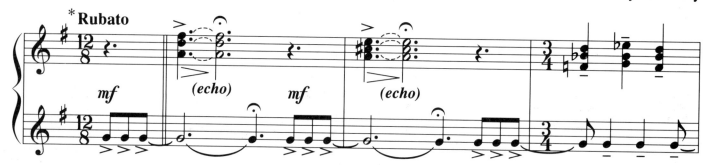

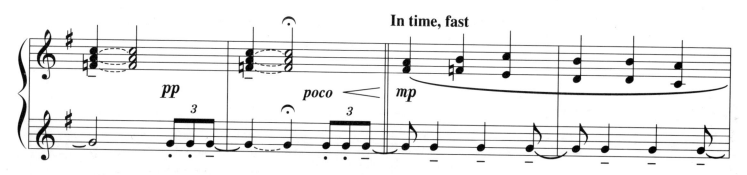

*Note: This piece goes back and forth frequently between *duple* and *triple* meter. In all cases, the eighth note remains the same value.

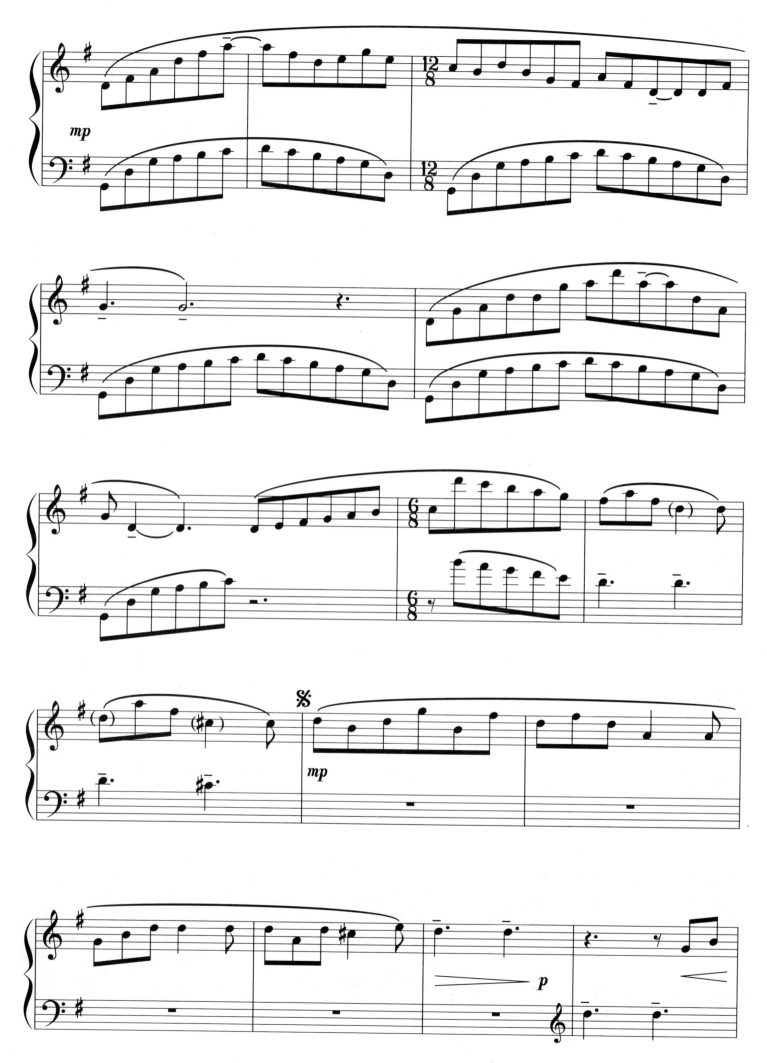

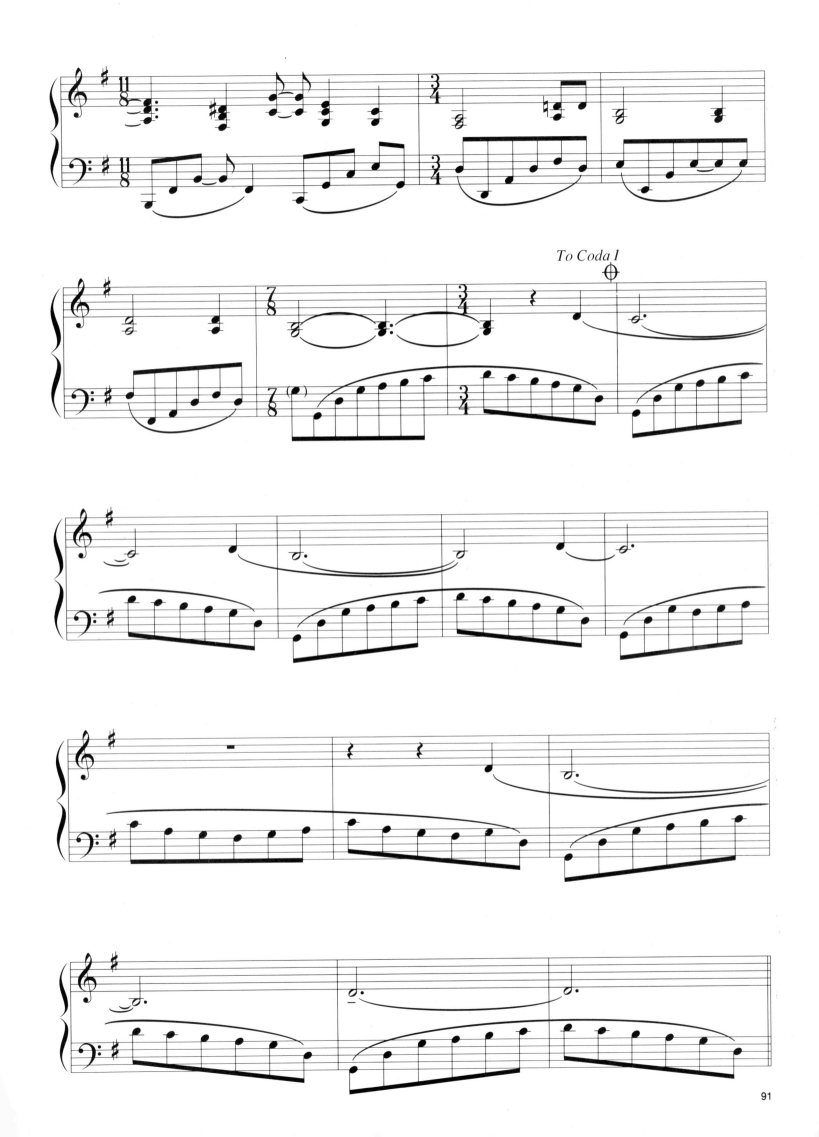

To Coda I

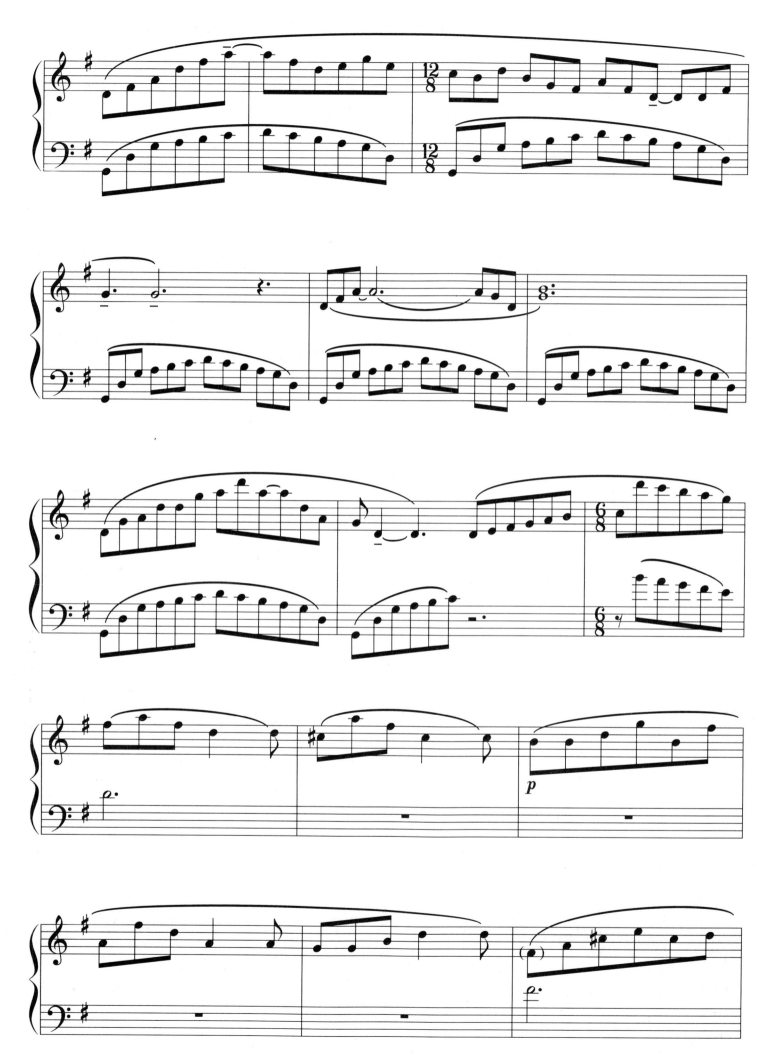

poco <

D.S. al Coda I

%

Coda I

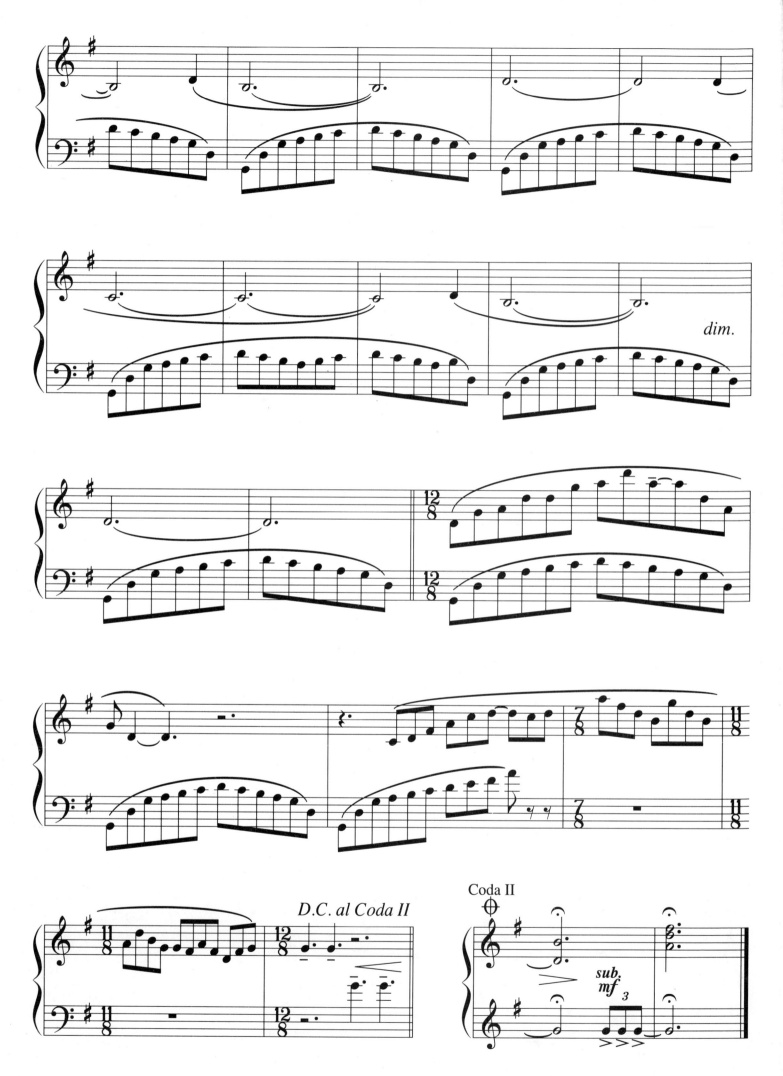